SIMPLE WEAVING

SIMPLE WEAVING

BY

ELSIE MOCHRIE

(of the Dryad Handicrafts)

THE DRYAD PRESS
LEICESTER

FIRST PUBLISHED, 1927
SECOND REVISED EDITION, 1932
THIRD EDITION, REVISED AND ENLARGED, 1934
FOURTH REVISED EDITION, 1936

CONTENTS

INTRODUCTION

Weaving is a basic craft which until recently was considered unsuitable for schools because elaborate apparatus was necessary. Fortunately, by the efforts of a few interested workers this idea has been proved wrong. By studying primitive methods of weaving, various kinds of simple apparatus have been evolved based on the crude but efficient looms fashioned by the early weavers. Our City of Leicester can claim its full share in this. The small loom upon which this booklet is based was first used in the Leicester School of Art some years ago and has since found its way into many schools. Its success is no doubt due to its efficiency, for it is in no way 'gadgety' like some of the looms one sees in use and, therefore, allows for full concentration on the actual weaving without any difficulties of manipulation due to a too often badly constructed loom. Undoubtedly some good results may be obtained by other methods, but the time and patience involved is hardly justifiable considering the limited time it is possible to devote to craftwork of any kind in schools.

Weaving provides one of the great necessities of life, and is, therefore, a real craft and not merely a 'stunt' like some of the so-called crafts practised in schools to-day. By its practice children will learn something of the qualities essential in a good piece of woven material, and should thus become competent to distinguish between reliable and shoddy materials. It should develop good taste and judgment in the matter of colour and design, both of vital importance in everyday life.

Handweaving should not be an excuse for slovenly work. The old Egyptians are said to have woven finer cloth than can be produced to-day by machinery. The loom recommended has the advantage of producing pieces of weaving which can be made into useful things instead of being mere exercises, a most important item in all craftwork.

SIMPLE WEAVING

A piece of woven material is composed of two sets of threads called the warp and weft. The warp threads run lengthwise of the material at right angles to the weft threads, the latter being threaded under and over the warp threads, forming a web. In order to do this satisfactorily it is necessary to stretch the warp threads on a frame or loom.

When weaving is taught as a school craft it must be graded. The younger children use simple cardboard looms for the first stages. These are economical and serve excellently for teaching the principles of weaving, and will therefore be dealt with here first.

CARD LOOM WEAVING FOR INFANTS

No. 1 Looms

The simplest of the cardboard looms are square or rectangular, being cut from a piece of stiff cardboard with a serrated edge at the top and bottom, about 5 in. by 3½ in. and 6 in. square, or a little larger, as preferred. The warp thread is wound on one side of the card between and round the serrations.

Fairly thick cotton (the kind used for knitting) is an excellent inexpensive material to use on these first cardboard looms. Four-ply wool is equally suitable, but costs a little more; raffia can also be used, although the uneven thickness of the strands is perhaps not quite so easily managed by the very young children.

The end of the cotton is tied to the first serration at the top left-hand corner (A in illustration, Plate 2). It is taken down

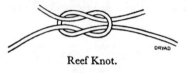

Reef Knot.

the card and round behind serration B at the bottom, then up the card and round serration C at the top, and so on, the final end being tied round the last serration. New lengths of cotton are joined on with a reef knot. (It should hardly be necessary, however, with the smaller looms.) The knot is made as follows: hold the old end in the left hand and the new one in the right; tie the left end over the right end. The ends will then have exchanged places; tie the present right end over the left end.

The weaving is carried out with a needle in the manner of darning, starting at the bottom right-hand corner, picking up one strand and missing one alternately, and then returning in the next row in a similar manner, picking up the threads missed in the first row, and so on. A long weaving needle is recommended (see L, Plate 2). Each successive row is pressed down into position close to the previous row with the fingers, but not so close that the warp strands are hidden entirely. Care must be taken not to pull the weft thread too tight or the edges of the weaving will be drawn in.

When a new length of weft thread is required, it is woven under the few last used warp strands so that the old and new ends overlap, making them secure when the next row is pressed down into position.

It will be noticed that in weaving on these cards the mesh is not square, i.e. a greater amount of the weft thread is showing than the warp. This is due to the wide spacing of the warp threads, which makes the weaving easier at this stage.

The weaving is removed from the card by easing the loops of warp off the serrations so that with care the looms can be used again.

These small pieces of weaving need not be treated as mere exercises, for they can be made into such simple articles as needle books, kettle holders, lunch bags, etc., sewing two pieces together where necessary.

No. 2 Looms

The next form of card loom has a series of dots marked along the top and bottom edges of the card. These are pierced either with a small awl (M, Plate 2) or a needle, and take the place of the serrations, being arranged in a zig-zag manner, as shown in Illustrations I and J. This is to allow the warp strands to be placed closer together (without weakening the loom) so that a square mesh will be obtained in the finished weaving, i.e. equal portions of warp and weft showing, as in weaving later on a wooden loom.

A needle (N, Plate 2) is used to insert the warp threads through the dots. Beginning at the dot D (illustration, Plate 2), tie a knot in the end of the cotton and come up through D, across the loom and down through E, up through F and across and down through G, up through H and so on, tying the final end to the short stitch on the underside.

The weaving is carried out in a similar manner to that on the previous cards. Presuming that a long weaving needle is being used, it is helpful at some stage to suggest to the children that when they have woven entirely across one row, before drawing the needle through, they should raise it up a little to show the space between the set of warp strands above the needle and the set below it. Then similarly in the next row to point out how the two sets of threads have changed places. This will help considerably later on in weaving on a larger wooden loom.

Some experiments with colour can be made by introducing bands of contrasting colour in some definite sequence, such as Illustration I. Then, following this, two or three colours can be used in the warp, i.e. when a group of the first colour has been inserted, join on a second colour with a reef knot on the back of the card, and continue thus alternately. The number of holes in the loom must be counted and divided first accordingly. If these colours are used for the weft in the same order and proportion a plaid pattern will be obtained (see Illustration J).

When finer cotton or wool is to be used, cards with three lines of holes are used so that the warp strands can be placed sufficiently close together to obtain a square mesh. Illustration K shows this with simple patterns obtained by weaving alternate rows of two colours, etc.

To remove the weaving, when completed, tear the card away along the holes and finish off the weaving neatly by oversewing.

No. 3, Shaped Card Looms

At this stage some useful articles can be made on looms, following some particular shape. Here, instead of the weaving being
horizontal, across vertical warp strands as on the previous
looms, it is for the most part circular or semicircular, with
the warp strands radiating from a given point, this being either
a hole in the card or a small brass ring attached to the card.
The shape of the article is marked with dots spaced at equal
distance apart, usually about ⅜ in., and the warp strands are
taken from the hole or ring through the dots. Mats, bags, egg
and tea cosies, slippers, etc., can be made in this way, as shown
on the upper half of Plate 4. Four-ply wool and raffia are the
most suitable materials to use, with fine macrame string in
some instances for the warp—because it is firmer, e.g. for the
slipper, it helps to keep its shape better during wear. Warp
strands are joined as before with a reef knot.

The looms for the articles mentioned above are shown on
Plate 3; all of them can be bought ready marked. For circular
and oval mats the warp thread is brought down through a
dot and up through the centre hole, down through the next
dot, up through the hole, and so on, tying the final end to the
first end. The weaving is started close to the centre hole and
carried on continuously until the warp strands are filled. With
oval mats a few extra rows are required at the ends to fill
them. The surplus card is torn away along the holes, and the
edges finished by sewing a group of strands over them.

The bags and cosies have two brass rings sewn one on each
side of the card at the same point. The end of the warp is tied
to one of the rings and threaded through the first dot B to
the other side of the card and then into the second ring. From
here back through the second dot C and into the first ring
again, and so on until all the dots have been used, when the
final end is tied to one of the rings. The weaving is started
close to the ring in each case, and carried to and fro as before,
pressing each row down to the previous row. A shorter needle
(O, Plate 2) is more convenient for curved weaving.

In the bags, when the top portion as far as the first two
dots is woven, the two outer warp strands will be filled, so

that these are omitted and the weaving carried on between the next two strands, and so on, omitting the strands in pairs as they become filled.

The slippers are made with a combination of straight and semicircular weaving which can be seen from the loom on Plate 3, warped ready for weaving. The warp strands for the sides of the slipper are threaded between two sets of dots while those at the toe are from one set of dots into a ring.

Various colour schemes can be adopted from the experience gained on the previous card looms. The warp can be of more than one colour if desired, introducing a plaid pattern. This will only show as such, however, where the warp strands are close enough together. As they widen out to the shape of the article the weaving will look like that on the first card looms, with very little of the warp showing.

In addition to the pattern made by the introduction of contrasting colours, experiments may be made by picking up more than one warp strand, e.g. picking up two and missing one or two, and so on, weaving two or three rows in this manner.

Sufficient knowledge of the principles and possibilities of weaving should have been acquired from the foregoing card looms to enable the children to proceed to something more advanced. A simple type of board loom which is a permanent apparatus may be used before passing on to the next stage. On this loom slightly longer lengths may be woven and made up into useful articles. When setting up the warp, the required number of threads are cut and tied round the loom, two strands of 4-ply wool being passed through every dent in the cardboard spacing gauges which are supplied with the loom. A shed stick is inserted under alternate threads and tied from end to end with a piece of string.

A needle is used to carry the weft thread as when using the cardboard looms, but for alternate rows the shed stick is turned on its edge, thus lifting every other warp thread at once. As the work grows the warp is pulled evenly round the board and the weaving continued as before.

If desired the warp may be mounted in a continuous length.

To do this place a round rod, the width of the loom, along the outside edge at one end of the board. Tie the wool to the rod and wind round the loom, using the spacing gauges as before. Twist the wool round the rod and return in the opposite direction. Continue winding in this way from each direction, twisting the wool round the rod every time. If this is done it will keep the work even as it is pulled round the loom. So far, the weaving described has been done with a needle, which is of necessity rather slow and quite impractical for large pieces of weaving. Therefore it becomes necessary to introduce a larger wooden frame loom, which is used with a simple device for manipulating the warp strands in place of the needle.

A SIMPLE BRAID LOOM

A loom constructed in the form of a wooden frame, as shown in Diagram 1, is recommended. It offers many possibilities, for these looms are made in a variety of sizes, ranging from $3\frac{1}{2}$ in. to 7 in. wide, and onwards to 20 in., the wider looms being fitted with rollers, which will be dealt with later, so that materials of corresponding widths can be woven. They have been used in schools and by other workers for some time and have proved entirely satisfactory.

The loom is composed of four uprights connected in pairs at the two ends with four small rods round which the warp threads pass. The uprights are held firmly in position with two cross bars on each side fixed to the uprights at the corners and fastened together at the crossing points, as shown in the illustration. Woven braids up to 46 in. long can be made on these smaller looms, and suggestions for using the braids will be made later.

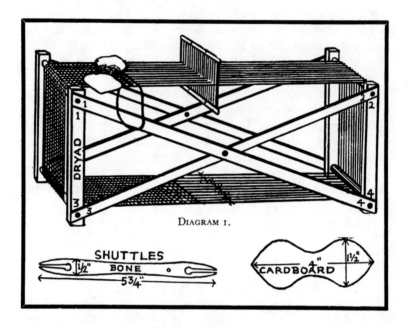

DIAGRAM 1.

THE HEDDLE

With these looms a device called a heddle is introduced for picking up the required warp threads across the entire width of the loom in one movement, effecting a great saving of time and energy compared with the previous use of a needle.

There are various types of heddles made of wire or sheet metal or of string attached to a wooden frame. The wire or metal heddles perform three operations. They regulate the warp strands and make the necessary division in the warp known as the shed, through which the shuttle containing the weft thread is passed, while they also serve as a beater to beat the rows of weaving together. The heddles illustrated on the looms are cut from sheet metal, and are called

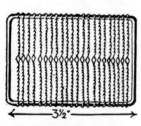

DIAGRAM 2. Wire Heddle.

Metlyx heddles. The slats are bored with large holes. They are smooth and pleasant to hold, and can be obtained with a chromium plated finish. The warp strands are threaded alternately through these eyelet holes and the intermediate spaces so that when the heddle is lifted up or pressed down, the opening or shed is formed through which the shuttle containing the weft thread is passed, i.e. the set of threads through the eyelet holes go up with the heddle when it is lifted and the threads through the spaces remain horizontal or vice versa when the heddle is pressed down.

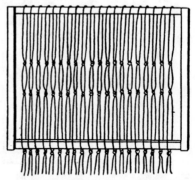

DIAGRAM 3. Frame with string heddles.

The wire heddle previously mentioned is shown in Diagram 2. This is composed of a series of hand-twisted wires which are arranged a small distance apart and fastened to a stout wire frame. Each of these twisted wires has a loop or small eyelet hole at the centre.

The string heddles attached to a wooden frame, shown in Diagram 3, being less rigid than the previous heddles, can only be used to *lift up* the warp strands, so that here two heddles are required, one to make each shed, and the warp threads which pass through the spaces in the previous heddles are passed through the holes in the second heddle and the two heddles lifted alternately.

These heddles are favoured by some teachers because they can be made at school, and, further, they are similar to the heddles used later on the large table and foot-power looms. On the other hand, they are not so convenient to use on these small looms, for, in addition to requiring two sets of heddles, this type of heddle cannot be used to beat the rows of weaving together, so that a coarse celluloid comb or flat wooden stick must be used.

There is little doubt that children will quickly realize the slight change in procedure in passing on to the larger looms where the heddle frames and the beater are fixed to the loom,

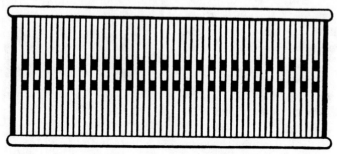

DIAGRAM 4. Rustless Steel Heddle.

and are thus more easily worked. It is, therefore, proposed to deal here with the more rigid type of heddle. There are other metal heddles which vary slightly in the making, but which are worked on exactly the same principle as the one previously described. Diagram 4 shows a better quality heddle recommended for use with the wider looms.

HEDDLE LOOM WEAVING

It may interest the worker to know that the rigid heddle is sometimes made to serve as a loom in itself for the making of braids, etc., without a framework to hold the warp. The heddles used in this method of weaving are often made of wood, which may be obtained in 3 ft. lengths, $\frac{1}{8}$ in. by $\frac{3}{16}$ in. and $\frac{5}{8}$ in. by $\frac{1}{8}$ in. The following notes on the construction of the heddle will be helpful.

Materials required: 4 lengths, $\frac{5}{8}$ in. by $\frac{1}{8}$ in. stripwood 9 in. long; 36 lengths, $\frac{1}{8}$ in. by $\frac{3}{16}$ in. stripwood $6\frac{3}{4}$ in. long; Panel pins; Glue.

Place two 9 in. strips of $\frac{5}{8}$ in. by $\frac{1}{8}$ in. stripwood on a work board and tack at the ends to hold in position $5\frac{1}{2}$ in. apart.

Commencing at one end, glue each $6\frac{1}{2}$ in. slat of $\frac{1}{8}$ in. by $\frac{3}{16}$ in. stripwood in turn to the 9 in. strips (which will form the frame). To obtain even spaces between the slats, drive a panel pin into

PLATE 1. Braids woven at a weaving course for teachers at the Leicester College of Art.

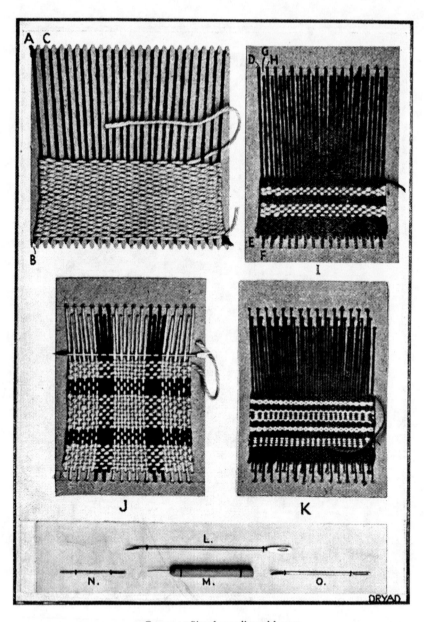

PLATE 2. Simple cardboard looms.

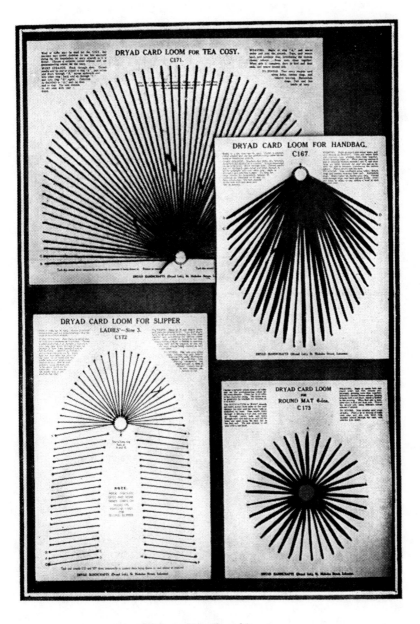

PLATE 3. Shaped card looms.

PLATE 4. Above: Articles made on shaped card looms.
Below: Ties woven on small braid looms.

the board after each one. Then brush a thin coat of glue across the portion of the slats already fixed to one side of the frame. Complete the frame by placing the two remaining 9 in. strips into position and secure by driving in panel pins at the corners and also at intervals across the frame. Put under weights until dry.

When dry, place a piece of stiff cardboard under the slats for support and carefully mark the position for the holes by drawing a line across the centre of the heddle. Then drill a hole through each slat, and to obtain a smooth finish to the holes a heated pin may be used.

Setting up the warp when weaving without a loom is a very simple matter. The worker is advised to fix two warp posts or pegs the full length of the warp apart and to wind the required number of threads round the posts—each time round counting as two warp threads. Then to cut the warp at one peg and loop each pair at the uncut end round a thick rod not less than 10 in. long, and finish with a single thread. A notch is made in the rod a short distance away from each end and a length of string tied round the notches. It is then tied or hung to some fixed point.

The heddle is then threaded as already described with the outer strand at each selvedge passing through a hole, and the warp tied in groups to a second rod, which is in turn attached to the waist or belt of the worker, who sits at the required distance to give the necessary tension to the warp for weaving.

The weft thread is wound on a shuttle and the heddle operated as previously mentioned. As the weaving progresses, it is drawn forward round the rod over a piece of stiff paper and held in position at each end with a drawing pin.

There is an old Norwegian method of weaving braids in a somewhat similar manner, which is still practised in some countries to-day. Here, however, the weft thread is pulled tight so that the warp strands are drawn close together and the weft thread is completely hidden. Thus it is necessary to use a striped warp to obtain pattern. Either the shuttle or a separate flat stick is used to press the rows of weft thread close together, as here it would be impossible to use the heddle for this purpose owing to the difference in width.

B

"INKLE" LOOM

A copy of a traditional Scottish braid loom is illustrated above. The loom is fitted with fixed leashes and the shed is made by alternately lifting and depressing, by hand, the threads which are between the leashes. It is interesting to note that this method of weaving is the reverse of that followed when using a rigid heddle. Whereas the threads through the spaces of a heddle are always level, in this method these are the threads which are moved up and down by hand to produce the sheds and those through the leashes held in position. To make this possible it will be seen that the threads through the leashes are passed over a grooved peg at a higher level.

Most pleasing warp effects may be produced and the braids used as belts or joined to make shopping bags, rugs, etc.

MATERIALS

Having discussed the loom and various types of heddles the next important item is the materials for weaving. In elementary work on the cardboard looms, coarse cotton, four-ply wool and raffia are generally used, as already stated, while for the wooden looms with heddles two-and three-ply wool or cottons of a corresponding size are used.

The twisted wire heddles are a little finer than the Metlyx ones, allowing for thirteen to fourteen threads to every inch in the width of the weaving, which makes it possible to use two- or three-ply wool. The Metlyx heddles give twelve threads to the inch, and are, therefore, most suitable for three-ply wool. This calculation is termed the dentage, and a heddle is described as having 'so many' dents to the inch.

The wool used must have a smooth surface and be fairly tightly twisted to withstand any friction or strain to which it may be subjected while on the loom. Loosely twisted wools will tend to fluff during the weaving.

The weft thread can be softer and more loosely twisted, being either of the same thickness as the warp or a little thicker if heavier material is required. A fine thread can be used double either for the warp or weft, in which case the weft thread is wound double on the shuttle. Where cotton is used on the wider looms a medium-sized cotton used double for the warp and weft makes a very pleasant material which is firmer than that woven with single coarse cotton. The latter is more suitable for weaving the narrow braids.

Wool is most favoured for the beginner, no doubt due to its elasticity, which makes it easy to manipulate. Mercerised cottons are generally preferred to the duller finish, as they give more sparkle to the finished weaving.

COLOUR

Colour is important in weaving. Well-chosen colours, pleasingly combined, are a keynote to the success of the finished work, and it is here that part of the value of weaving lies as a school craft. Use only one or two colours at first, until the process

of weaving has been grasped, as then the possibilities and
effects of the combination of various colours in the weaving
will be much better realized: e.g., in making a simple braid
of two colours, one colour for the warp and one for the weft,
where two distinct contrasting colours are used, such as black
and white, a speckled effect will result; whereas if two blending
colours of equal strength, such as blue and purple, are chosen,
the result will be a rich glow of broken colour. For the main
part, or groundwork, of a braid or a wider piece of weaving
the last-mentioned is very successful, with small bands of
sharply contrasting colours introduced at regular intervals to
form the pattern. Two tones of the same colour, one for the
warp and one for the weft, also give an interesting groundwork,
or, when preferred, the same colour can be used for both
warp and weft. Further interest is sometimes given to the
weaving if more than one colour is used for the warp. The
colours can be arranged in stripes in some definite order, so
that with the other colours used in the weft the finished weaving
has the appearance of a plaid pattern, as shown in the scarf
on Plate 12.

An interesting experiment, which is recommended, was
made at the Leicester College of Art on one of the wider looms.
(It would be practical on the 5½ in. onwards.) The primary
colours, yellow, red, and blue, were used in groups for the warp
and then crossed with the same colour in similar bands for the
weft. The result was most effective and instructive, being a
practical application of the mixing of the primary colours to
make the secondaries. Allowance, of course, had to be made
for the difference between the interweaving of coloured *wools*
and the intermixing of coloured *pigments*, the tone of the
secondaries varying somewhat accordingly.

PUTTING THE WARP ON THE LOOM

The position of the warp strands has already been mentioned
in the description of the loom, i.e. through the heddle and
round the four small rods. The strands must all be of an even
tension and taut if the weaving is to be regular. This is simpli-

fied if the centre warp strand is put on first and the strands on
either side of this added alternately, as the weight of the heddle
will thus be kept central. Begin, then, with the centre warp strand
at one of the small rods (the one nearest to you). Thread it
through the eyelet hole nearest the centre of the heddle (a
crochet hook is useful for drawing the threads through), round
the second, third and fourth rods, and back to the first, where
it is securely tied with a reef-knot on this rod. In the first stage
of the knot loop one end *twice* round the other end instead of
the customary once, as this helps to keep the thread from slipping while tying the second stage of the knot, so that the strand
is made taut. Keep the heddle close up to the second rod, so
that it will not sag the threads. Add the warp strand on each
side of the centre strand in the same way. These will pass
through the spaces in the heddle; the next will pass through
an eyelet hole, and so on until the warp strands are complete.
The number of warp strands depends on the width of the
braid required. The whole width of the heddle need not
necessarily be used, but the outer strands should pass through
a hole and not a space, as this gives a better edge to the weaving.
It must be noted that the width of the finished weaving is
always less than the width of the warp threads in the heddle,
e.g. in this size loom there is a difference of ½ in., while in
the larger looms the difference is greater in proportion.

During the process of weaving, as the warp strands at the
top of the loom become used a new supply is brought forward
by drawing the strands round the loom. With wool this is
quite a simple matter, but with cotton, which has not the same
elasticity, there is a tendency for the strands to close up and
spoil the weaving. This can be avoided, however, by placing
a flat stick or ruler at one end of the loom outside the uprights
before tying the first warp strand and keeping it thus throughout
the completion of the warp. Then, when the weaving is started
and ready to be moved round, the stick is removed so that
the warp is then sufficiently slack to be moved gently round
without disturbing the fabric. When this has been done the
stick is slipped back into position again and the warp is once
more taut, ready for proceeding with the weaving.

TO WEAVE

Before starting to weave, the weft thread must be wound on a shuttle. One shuttle is required for each colour. The shuttles can be cut from stiff cardboard the size and shape shown below Diagram 1 on page 14. For the 5½-in. and 7-in. looms they would require to be a little larger. Small bone ones, which are also shown, can be used if preferred or, alternatively, wooden shuttles may be obtained for use with the wider looms. They must be wound evenly and flatly so that they will pass easily through the shed.

To commence weaving, hold the loom in position between the body and the edge of a table, as shown in Plate 5.

Begin about 3 in. from the knots on the first bar, as this distance will allow for a good shed to be made. If desired, the 3 in. can be used to serve as a fringe later. Press the heddle down with the left hand and pass the shuttle through the shed with the right, drawing the weft thread through until only a small end remains. Now lift the heddle with the right hand and pass the shuttle through with the left, drawing the thread through again, at the same time pressing it close to the first line of weaving with the heddle. There is sometimes an inclination to press or beat the rows of weaving too closely together, so that the warp strands are almost hidden. In good weaving an equal amount of the warp and weft strands should be visible, so that a square mesh is formed (see Plates 6 and 7).

The width of the weaving must be kept uniform and the edges regular. At the beginning there may be a tendency to pull the thread too tightly, but this is soon rectified with a little practice. Continue the weaving in this way, alternately pressing down and lifting the heddle and passing the weft thread through the shed made.

As already mentioned, when the weaving approaches the second rod and it is no longer possible to make a good shed through which to pass the shuttle, it must be moved round the loom so that a new supply of warp is obtained. Take hold of the warp strands firmly and pull them round towards the first rod until the last row of weaving is about 3 in. from this rod. Repeat this process as required until the weaving is completed, continuing as near to the commencing knots of the warp strands as the making of the shed will allow. If the warp strands are of wool they may stretch a little during the weaving and become loose, in which case they can be tightened by inserting a ruler between the strands and the uprights of the second rod, as previously suggested for a cotton warp. When the weaving is complete, cut the warp strands along the row of knots to remove it from the loom. The finishing of the ends of the warp is described later.

JOINING

When it is necessary to introduce a new weft thread in the narrow braids made on the 3½ in. and 5-in. looms, the new thread is passed through the same shed as the last row of weaving, so that there are two rows through the same shed across the entire width of the braid.

In the 7-in. looms, and later in the wider looms, it is not necessary for the two threads to overlap across the whole width of the weaving, and is less noticeable as follows.

After weaving the last row with the old weft thread, change the shed ready to proceed with the next row and thread the old end through the shed for a distance of 1 in. Then introduce the new weft thread, beginning at the edge in the usual way. The old and new weft threads will thus overlap for 1 in. and be quite secure, so that the surplus ends can be cut off.

PATTERN WEAVING

The simplest form of pattern making is that of introducing colour in bands in some regular sequence, still continuing with the weaving in the ordinary way, i.e. with the weft thread passing over one warp strand and under one alternately throughout, changing the shed after each row, as already described. This is termed plain or 'tabby' weaving, and is illustrated in braid A on Plate 6. The other form of pattern making consists of actual variation of the weaving in addition to the colour arrangement, where the weft thread passes over more than one strand in some definite sequence according to the pattern decided upon. Sometimes it may pass through the same shed two or three times without changing the shed. A number of these patterns are shown in the braids B, C, D and E, on Plates 6, 7 and 8.

Twills are produced by passing the weft thread, of a contrasting colour to the warp, under and over one, two or three warp threads, moving by step of one warp thread in each row either to the right or to the left.

Block patterns are obtained by passing the weft thread under and over groups of warp strands in order and by repeating the pattern rows with a row of tabby weaving after each pattern row. A contrasting colour is frequently used for the pattern rows, although in some instances the pattern can be woven in the same colour as that used for the plain weaving or background, but usually it is not so effective. Two strongly contrasting colours were used here for illustration purposes, namely, orange and black, but the effect can be softened by using two more evenly balanced colours.

The patterns are first planned or 'drafted' out on squared graph paper, using each tiny square to represent one warp and one weft strand. The patterns in braid C on Plate 7 are shown drafted out in this way in diagram form on page 27. The plain row between each pattern row is omitted for convenience, as the effect of the pattern can be much better judged by so doing, and actually it shows very little in the finished weaving. As a further guide to the worker, patterns 9 and 10 are given later in detail so that they can be followed in conjunction with the drafted patterns. After studying these the worker should find it quite a simple matter to follow the remaining patterns and be able later to plan out further patterns of her own making.

In weaving the pattern rows the heddle is used only as a beater. The warp threads required for the pattern are picked up either with the shuttle or, alternatively, a ruler is used and turned on its edge to make the shed through which the shuttle is passed.

When weaving a narrow braid after planning the pattern the warp strands should be counted and divided up into the

PLATE 5. Showing the position of the loom in use.

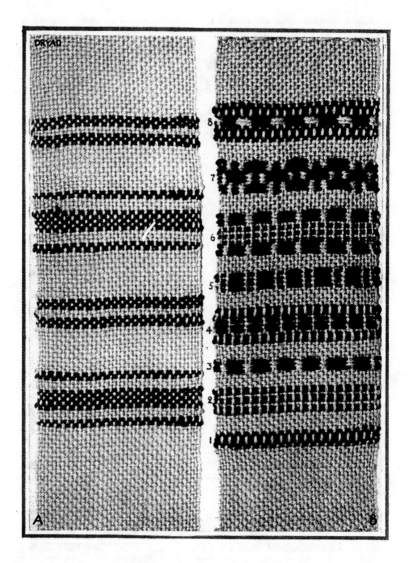

PLATE 6. Braids A and B, showing some simple patterns.

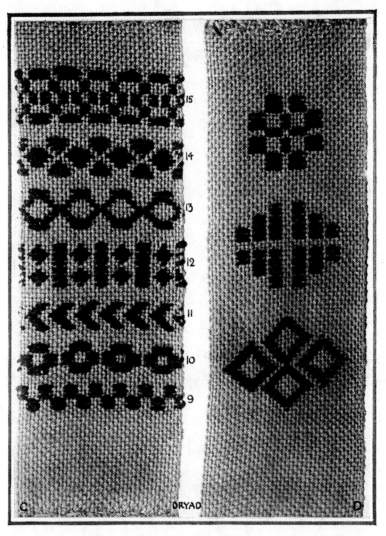

PLATE 7. Braid C, woven patterns, shown also in draft form on page 27.
Braid D, showing examples of inlay patterns.

PLATE 8. Examples of pattern weaving.

various groups accordingly, and any surplus strands arranged to come at the beginning and end of the rows, so that they do not visibly interfere with the balance of the pattern. This will be seen on examining braids B and C, and in describing these patterns the threading of the actual pattern therefore commences from the first star. These braids were woven on a $3\frac{1}{2}$-in. loom, using the full width of the wire heddle, which made forty-one strands altogether.

BRAID B. (Illustrated on Plate 6.)

This introduces some very simple patterns, including 'bar' patterns made by passing the weft thread three or four times through the same shed. A greater number of times is not recommended, as the weaving would be loose and impractical. This type of pattern looks well repeated at definite intervals in plain weaving or combined with other patterns.

Pattern 1

Weave one plain row with black wool, change the shed, or heddle, and weave another row. Then with the heddle in the same position weave two more rows, each time either going under or over the first warp strand to prevent the weaving from coming undone. Change the shed again, and weave another row to complete the pattern.

Pattern 2

This is a variation of the first pattern. Weave one row of black, then with the heddle in the same position weave another row. Change the shed, and weave a row with the orange wool. Repeat from the beginning twice.

Pattern 3

In this pattern there are no plain rows in between the pattern rows, and the heddle is not used. Thread the black wool over two warp strands, * under two, over four, repeat from *. In the next row thread orange wool *under* the threads the black wool passed over, and over the threads it passed under. Repeat these two rows once and weave the black row again, making five rows altogether.

C

Pattern 4

Weave three rows with the heddle in the same position, using black wool, then change the shed and weave a plain row with orange wool. Next weave with the black wool under one and over three along the row, for three rows, continuing the weaving with orange wool between each row. Then weave three rows with the black wool without changing the shed to correspond with the beginning.

Pattern 5

This pattern is similar to pattern 3, and again the heddle is not used. Weave with the black wool over two, * under one, over one, under one, over four, repeat from *.

The next row is woven with the orange wool, passing under the threads the black passed over, and over the threads it passed under in the previous row. Repeat both black and orange rows twice, and then the black row again.

Pattern 6

The first five rows of this pattern are woven exactly the same as pattern 3. Then weave the orange and black in alternate rows of plain weaving, commencing with a row of orange, for seven rows. Finally, weave five rows the same as the first five.

Pattern 7

This is worked on the same principle as pattern 5 without making a shed. For the first row weave with black over three, * under two, over one, under two, over five, repeat from *. In the next row weave with orange under three, * over two, under one, over two, under five, repeat from *. Repeat these two rows and then again the first row, making five rows altogether, which completes the first group of blocks. For the sixth row take the black wool * over one, under two, over five, under two, repeat from *. The seventh row is worked with orange wool * under one, over two, under five, over two, repeat from *.

Repeat these two rows once, then work the sixth row again. This makes the centre group of black blocks which come above the small orange and black blocks of the previous group.

The next five rows are worked in the same way as the first five.

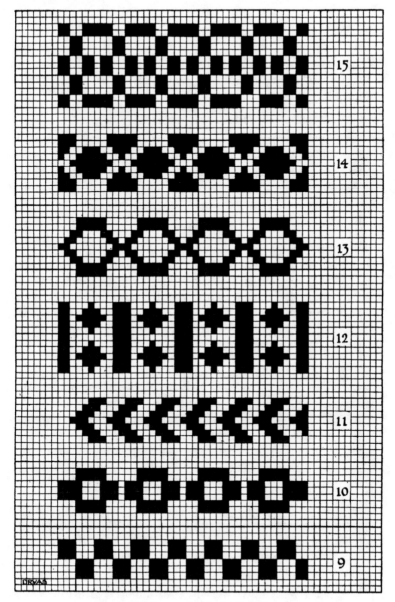

Draft of patterns in Braid C, Plate 7.

Pattern 8

This consists of pattern 1 and a pattern similar to No. 3. Weave pattern 1 with black wool, then weave under and over four threads with black and orange wool, three rows of black and two rows of orange arranged alternately, after which repeat pattern 1.

BRAIDS C AND D. (Illustrated on Plate 7.)

Braid C is shown in draft form on page 27, so that, as previously stated, only patterns 9 and 10 will be given in detail, as the others can then be followed from the draft. A plain row is woven between each pattern row, but this is omitted in the descriptions to save repetition.

The heddle is not used when threading the pattern rows.

Pattern 9

For this chequer pattern, pass the wool over three threads and under three threads along the row. Work three rows like this to complete the first row of squares. Then for the next row of squares thread the wool in a reverse position over the threads it passed under in the previous rows, working three rows to complete the pattern.

Pattern 10

Pass the wool under three threads, * over five, under five, repeat from *, and finish under three. Weave another row the same as this, and, for the next pattern row, thread the wool over four threads, * under three, over three, under one, over three, repeat from *, finishing over four threads. Work two more rows like this. The next two rows are the same as the first row.

BRAID D, illustrated on Plate 7, shows three examples of a slightly different form of pattern. Instead of the pattern extending the full width of the braid, as all the previous patterns do, it is woven in the centre portion of the braid only, in the following manner:

The plain weaving is worked continuously with the orange thread, and the black pattern thread is kept on the underside of the weaving and only used as required, thus the pattern is threaded or 'laid' in the braid, and so is given the name of Inlay pattern. This form of pattern is only suitable for narrow braids.

Woven Strip. (Illustrated on Plate 8.)

Here the weaving is wider and shows the full value of the repetition of the patterns across the width. All the patterns can be followed quite easily from the illustration. It would be quite good practice to make a draft of these patterns. A plain row is woven between each pattern row except in the narrow border lines of No. 5 pattern.

Further narrow braids are shown in Plate 1. These were pleated over in places to show as much pattern as possible.

SMALL ROLLER BRAID LOOM
Diagram 5

This loom is particularly suitable for school use as it is made collapsible to facilitate storage. It is made in the $3\frac{1}{2}$ in. size, similar to the previous braid loom, but is fitted with rollers in place of the upper rods. The surplus warp is wound round the back roller to be used as required, and the finished braid is wound on the front roller. The rollers are controlled by means of thumbscrews, which are fixed to the end of these. A piece of calico is nailed to each roller. A narrow stick is slotted into the hem at the edge of this and above the stick small slits are made in the calico at regular intervals. An additional warp stick is attached to the calico on both rollers by passing the string through the slits provided, leaving $\frac{1}{2}$ in. between the sticks and the calico. The warp threads will be attached to these sticks as described later.

These looms will hold three yards of warp, but less can be put on according to requirements. In calculating, allowance must be made for tying on and also for contraction and shrinkage, which take place when the weaving is damped and pressed.

The latter process is not essential in this narrow weaving, although it improves its appearance, but it is in the wider weaving, which is more likely to be subjected to hard wear. The amount to be allowed for tying, including the small portion at each end of the warp which cannot be woven, is approximately 12 in. on these small looms, with 3 in. to 4 in. on each

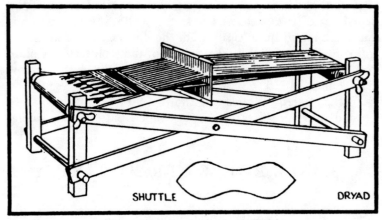

SHUTTLE   DRYAD

DIAGRAM 5. Small roller braid loom.

yard of warp for shrinkage. This is for wool—a little less can be allowed for cotton.

Having determined the length of the warp, the strands must be cut. A simple method of cutting them all of the same length is to insert two large nails in some convenient place or to fix two warp posts on a table half the distance of the required length apart, and then to wind the warp thread round these as many times as there are strands required for the width, so that when the strands are cut at one of the nails they are ready to put on the loom.

Here the threading of the heddle is completed before the warp is attached to either of the rollers of the loom, so that it can be conveniently done by resting the edge of the heddle on a table. When the threading is complete the strands are tied securely to the stick attached to the calico on the back roller in pairs.

The next process is to wind the warp on to the back roller. The thumbscrew is loosened and the strands wound on evenly and carefully by turning the roller, holding them taut while doing so. Where it is possible, this process is simplified if one person holds the warp taut while a second person turns the roller, placing a warp stick across the roller to protect the threads from the knots used when tying on, also winding in a few warp sticks at intervals throughout the length.

Sufficient warp must be left unwound to be carried over the loom and attached to the front roller. After tightening the thumbscrew of the back roller the strands are tied in small groups round the stick attached to the front roller. Each group is passed under and over the stick, divided into half and crossed underneath, *keeping all the strands at the same tension.* From here they are brought up and tied on top of the group with a reef-knot. When complete, if the warp is not sufficiently tight, adjust the rollers by means of the thumbscrews. The loom will then be ready for weaving, the process of which is exactly as described for the previous loom.

In this and all other roller looms it is advisable to place a spare warp stick through the first shed in the warp before commencing to weave. This helps to draw the warp threads together and to give a fine edge to the weaving.

As the weaving progresses and a fresh supply of warp is required, the thumbscrews of the rollers are loosened, and the finished weaving wound on the front roller until the last row of weaving is in a suitable position for continuing. At the same time a new supply of warp is unwound from the back roller. The thumbscrews are then tightened and the weaving continued.

When rolling the material on the front roller two or three thicknesses of brown paper should be included as before.

LARGER ROLLER BRAID LOOM
Diagram 6

This is also fitted with rollers, but, being a larger loom, namely, 9 in., 15 in., 18 in. or 20 in., the sides are made solid, so that it can be used as a table loom, instead of having to be held between the worker and a table. The making and putting on of the warp is also somewhat different. The increased number

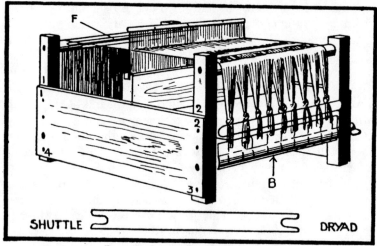

DIAGRAM 6. Larger roller braid loom.

of warp strands makes it necessary to use some means of keeping them in order across the additional width during the winding of the warp on to the roller and later in the weaving.

TO PREPARE THE WARP

The ideal way to make the warp is on a warping board, warping frame or warping posts (see Diagram 7), but if the worker does not possess any of this apparatus a substitute can be made, as mentioned later.

The WARPING BOARD, page 33, is about 6 ft. long by 1 ft. broad, and will make a warp up to 10 yards long. It is fitted with a number of removable pegs on which the warp is wound.

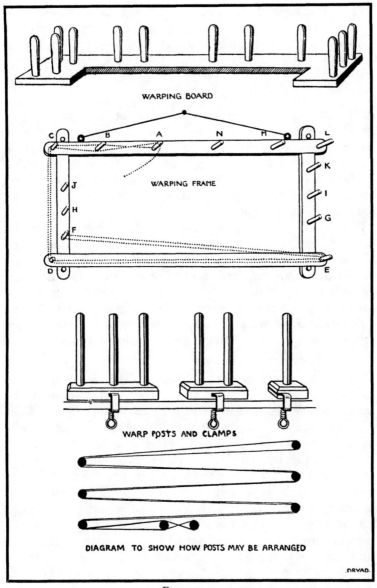

DIAGRAM 7.

The WARPING FRAME is made on exactly the same principle as the board, the difference being that the pegs are inserted into a frame instead of the board. It is made to hang on a wall and can be taken to pieces when not in use and stored in a cupboard. It measures 1 yard long by half a yard wide, and will make a warp up to 7½ yards long.

WARPING POSTS. These posts can be obtained made singly or made in groups of twos and threes. The posts are similar to the pegs used with the board and frame, with the addition of a clamp fixed at the bottom of the peg. This makes it possible to fix the posts on a table or convenient ledge in a position corresponding to the pegs, making an inexpensive substitute for the board or frame.

The following instructions are given for the warping frame, but they can be used for any of the apparatus described. First count the holes and spaces in the heddle to obtain the number of warp strands required, arranging as before for the outer strands to pass through a hole in the heddle, as this gives a better edge. It should be noted that this will necessitate an odd number of warp strands. If the whole width is not required, omit an equal number of holes and spaces at each end of the heddle.

A SELVEDGE can be made if desired as follows: After calculating the number of warp threads required, add six more, three for each edge, and then in threading the heddle make the last three warp strands on each side double. It is not essential in this type of loom, where the weaving is moderately coarse and consequently firm, but is preferred by some workers.

The thread to be warped should be wound into a ball or placed on a revolving skein winder. It is really advisable, and much more expedient, to use two balls, or put two skeins on the winder in making the warp. If balls are used they should be put into a receptacle of some kind so that the threads will unwind freely. It may not be necessary to use all the pegs on the frame to make a warp for this type of roller loom, as six yards is the maximum length of warp the loom will hold. The length of warp required is first determined, allowing for the tying and shrinkage, and then the pegs are used accordingly. In these larger looms 20 in. should be added for the tying, plus 3 in. to 4 in. for shrinkage on every yard. For example, to make a scarf, a warp about 90 in. long is usually put on the loom. Tie the ends of the two warp threads into a loop and slip the loop over peg A on the frame in diagram. Guide the threads to the left over peg B and along to peg C, round this and along to D, from here on to E and across to F. This will give sufficient length for the warp required. From F carry the threads back round the same pegs to C and from here *under* B and *over* and round A. This will form a cross in the threads between the pegs A and B, which is very important, for it is this that regulates the warp and keeps it in order. Repeat the process just described, carrying the threads to and fro between pegs A and F, making the cross between A and B, until the required amount of threads has been warped. To keep count of the threads during the process of warping tie them together with a length of string or wool on the inside of peg F in equal groups of approximately ten strands, i.e. three double strands from one side and two double strands from the other. The number of strands in the group should really be a factor of the total, for if done in this way there will be little difficulty in determining when the warp is complete.

By using two threads as suggested to make the warp, this will of necessity make the total an even number of warp strands, but, as previously stated, an odd number is required for threading the heddle. Therefore, before passing round the frame for the last time break off one of the threads and tie it round the first peg A, and then proceed with the other thread to the last peg F and secure this also, or vice versa, according to the number of strands required.

When it is necessary to make a longer warp, the length of the warp is extended by passing across from F to G, from G to H, H to I, I to J, J to K, and from here to L, M and N, or omitting some of the last pegs, according to the length required.

Before taking off the warp secure the cross made in the strands between pegs A and B by tying it with string. Thread a piece of string down one side of the cross, behind it and up the other side, and then tie the ends on top of the cross. Also tie a piece of string through the loops at each of the pegs A and F. Slip the warp from peg F first and loop it up in the form of a crochet chain with the right hand until the entire warp is removed.

If the worker does not possess any of the apparatus mentioned, the pegs can be substituted by long nails driven into a wall or board.

TO PUT THE WARP ON THE LOOM

Before proceeding to put the warp on the loom, two sticks are inserted in the cross in place of the string, one on each side of it, to preserve it and to allow the warp to be spread across the width of the loom. These two sticks are termed 'shed sticks' and are a little longer than the maximum width of the warp and are provided at the ends with small holes, through which they are tied together with string about ½ in. apart.

The heddle is placed in the groove provided on the loom, so that it is in position ready for threading with the warp. The string tied through the end of the warp nearest the cross is now removed and the loops slipped on to the fingers of the left hand. These loops must now be put through the heddle from the front towards the back roller, four threads, i.e. two loops into every other space of the heddle, thus leaving two holes and one space between. This threading is only a temporary one, so that the warp can be arranged fairly evenly across the loom in readiness for winding it on the back roller. (The heddle is threaded for weaving later.)

It is much easier for two people to do the threading, one to hold the loops and pass them to the other person, who takes them by means of a crochet or threading hook through the heddle to the back, where a stick is inserted to prevent them slipping back through the heddle. Special care must be taken not to twist the loops when passing them through the heddle. When this has been done the stick is securely attached to the roller at regular intervals by tying it with string through the slits provided in the strip of calico attached to the roller. The thumbscrew at the end of the roller is now loosened and the warp wound on. This must be done carefully and evenly, one person turning the roller and the other guiding the warp. Flat wooden sticks, known as warp sticks, are inserted at the beginning to protect the warp from the knots of string made when tying the stick to the calico and again later to separate the layers of warp. After turning the roller round once insert a warp stick over the knots and then gradually turn the roller round again, inserting two or three more sticks side by side. Then proceed to wind the remainder of the warp, inserting the remaining warp sticks at intervals, with the exception of two, throughout the length of the warp, leaving sufficient to reach to the front of the loom. Now the cross in the warp must be transferred from its present position in front of the heddle to the back of the heddle, as otherwise it would interfere with the weaving. Tighten the thumbscrew on the back roller so that the warp is taut. Untie the strings securing the ends of the sticks which hold the cross and turn the back stick nearest the heddle on its edge, thus making a wider space or shed between the threads, which can be followed through to the back of the heddle. Place a temporary stick of the same length through this space at the back of the heddle, then place the back shed stick by the side of the temporary stick. This can then be removed and the back shed stick pushed along to the end of the loom. The process is now repeated with the front shed stick, again using the temporary stick, and then the shed sticks are secured with string at each end as before. The cross will now be in the position shown on the loom at F in Diagram 6.

When this has been done untie the string securing the free end of the warp, cut the loops and draw the threads out of the heddle. This is now rethreaded ready for weaving, passing the warp threads alternately through the eyelet holes and spaces, as already described. A stick is attached to the front roller B by tying it with string through the slits in the calico on this roller and then the ends of the warp strands are tied to this stick in groups, keeping an even tension throughout. If necessary the warp is tightened before starting to weave by regulating the thumbscrews. Here, again, the process of weaving is exactly the same, but larger wooden shuttles are used, as illustrated below the loom, the weft thread being wound lengthwise between the forked ends. For the method of introducing a new weft thread refer to page 23.

Should a warp strand break during the process of weaving, a new length of warp thread must be joined on to the broken strand behind the heddle and threaded through it in place of the old one. A pin is inserted in the finished weaving in line with the strand and the end wound round it. The weaving is then continued and the end darned into the weaving later.

The knot employed should be a weaver's knot, which is made as follows:

WEAVER'S KNOT

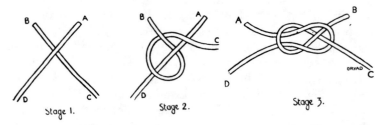

Stage 1.   Stage 2.   Stage 3.

Place the end of the broken strand A across the end of the new strand from left to right. Hold the strands at the crossing point between the thumb and finger of the left hand. With the right hand pass the long portion of the new strand C over the thumb, behind its end B and in front of the broken end A. Pass the short end A through the loop which is resting on the thumb—down between the thumb and first finger, and hold in position. Then to tighten the knot, pull the long strand marked C. Although these detailed instructions are necessary, when grasped, the tying of the knot is simple and speedy.

METHOD OF ESTIMATING THE QUANTITY
OF WOOL OR COTTON REQUIRED

Some suggestion as to how to estimate the amount of wool or cotton for a given length of material will no doubt be helpful.

Wool will be considered first. The following are the approximate lengths in 1 oz. of two-, three- and four-ply wool. These vary a little according to the make of wool.

   1 oz. two-ply equals 240 yards; 1 oz. three-ply equals 175 yards; 1 oz. four-ply equals 60 yards.

The first stage in calculating is to count the number of warp threads to be threaded in the heddle for the required width of weaving. Then, by dividing these by the number of yards in 1 oz., the amount required for 1 yard of warp will be obtained. For example, supposing there are 210 threads of two-ply wool required in the width, then $\frac{210}{240}$ oz. of wool will be required for 1 yard of warp, which equals $\frac{7}{8}$ oz. This, multiplied by the number of yards of warp required plus the amount to be allowed for tying on to the rollers and for shrinkage, will give the total amount for the warp.

The Weft requires a little more for each yard of weaving.

Cotton. As previously mentioned, a medium-sized cotton is used double on the wide looms for both warp and weft. This is calculated in a similar manner to the wool. There are approximately 800 yards of this size cotton in $\frac{1}{4}$ lb. cop. Here, however, the amount must be doubled for calculating to allow for the cotton being used double throughout.

SOME USES FOR THE BRAIDS

In offering suggestions for the use of the braids, attention is first given to those made on the small looms, as the narrow braids require a little more thought in making them into something useful than those made on the larger looms. Some of the articles suggested for the small looms can be made on the wider looms with less trouble, as the narrow braids have to be joined more frequently, but then all workers cannot have a large loom. Mention is made in each case with regard to this.

As already stated, wool is the easiest material for the beginner to use, so that, although mercerised cotton is given in some of the articles described, wool can be substituted if preferred.

The braids can be quite easily joined with a few embroidery stitches, which are described with some of the articles.

Each article is described as being made separately, but several can be made on the same warp where the same width of weaving is suitable. The length of the warp must, of course, be arranged accordingly. An entirely different appearance can be given to each article by varying the colours used for the weft.

It would not be possible in this small booklet to give a detailed description of the weaving of each article, i.e. the pattern rows and the order of the colours, but with the illustrations and description on pattern making already given it is hardly necessary. It is not suggested that the arrangement in the weaving of the articles should be copied exactly. Patterns arranged by the workers themselves will be far more valuable. The colours used are mentioned in most cases with regard to both the warp and weft.

In addition to the uses given for the narrow braids, they are very attractive used in the form of a trimming on a suitable material. For example, a cushion could be decorated with one or two strips of weaving on each side, a strip could be used along the bottom of a curtain, dresses and overalls could have a decoration round the neck and sleeves. The braids look best if they are sewn on at their edges with a few simple embroidery stitches, as this helps to soften the edges and connect the braids with the background material so that they are in harmony with it.

The simplest uses for the narrow braids are as a hat band, dress tie or belt, as with these no joining together is necessary. The ends of the warp strands can be made into a fringe by

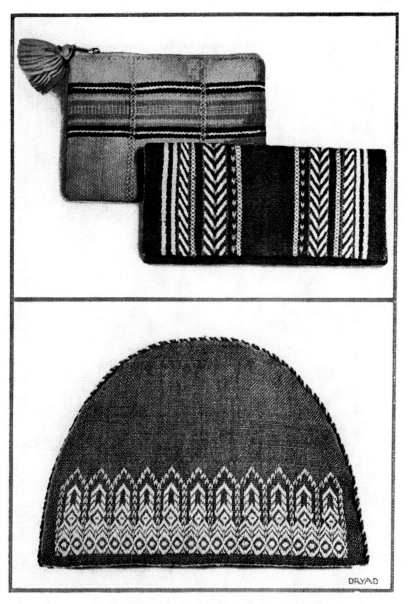

PLATE 9. Two Pochettes and a Tea Cosy. The lower pochette and cosy were woven at a weaving course for teachers at the Leicester College of Art.

DRYAD

PLATE 10. Above: Kettle Holder; Egg Cosy.
Below: Shoe Polisher; Pincushion.

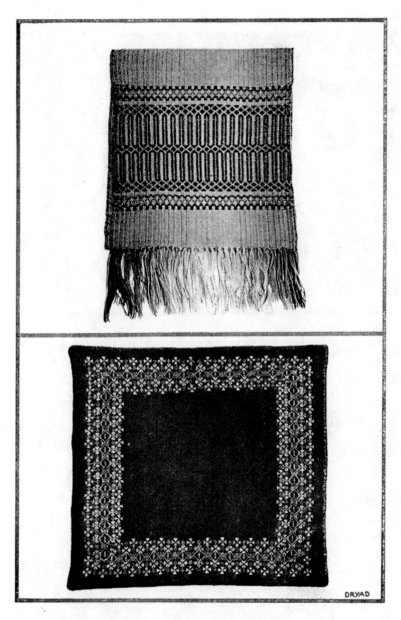

PLATE 11. Scarf and Cushion Cover.

Plaid Scarf.

PLATE 12.

Baby's Bonnet.

SOME USES FOR THE BRAIDS 41

knotting them together in groups of three or four quite close to the weaving. For a belt the ends of the braid can be hemmed and two buttonholed loops of wool added at one end, with two wooden beads at the other for a fastening, or, if preferred, a buckle can be introduced.

TIES can be made with a narrowing at the centre. This, of course, must be arranged during the weaving. When approximately 13 in. has been woven for the short end of the tie, the weft thread is gradually drawn in during the next few rows to the required width and continued thus for 15 in. A ruler or stick must be used to beat up the rows of weaving in place of the heddle. When complete, the weaving is gradually broadened out to its original width and 17 in. to 18 in. woven for the long end of the tie.

The ends of the tie can be secured with a row of hemstitching worked round the warp strands and into the weaving, as this will lie flatter than the knotting of the strands previously mentioned. Three-ply wool is recommended for tie-making. Artificial silk of the same thickness can be introduced. Thirty-one warp strands give a useful tie width of 2⅛ in., and these can be varied in colour if desired. Plate 4 shows some ties (three with a narrowing) worn by Sir Francis Acland, M.P., who, when giving the prizes at Lindisfarne College, Westcliff, told the boys how he made his own neckties in his spare time.

Plate 10 shows a few useful articles to make by joining the braids: a kettle-holder, egg cosy, shoe polisher and pin-cushion. Short lengths of braid can be made into a cover for a needle book or a spectacle cleaner, the ends being turned under and buttonholed with wool. The braid is folded into half and two or three pieces of flannel or chamois inserted. A child's purse can be made from a 9-in. length of braid by buttonholing the ends, folding it into three and sewing up the side edges.

KETTLE-HOLDER. (Illustrated on Plate 10.)

Two pieces of braid are woven on the small loom, using the entire width of the heddle, each piece being 11 in. long. The weaving can be done in one continuous length and cut into two pieces afterwards. Care must be taken to repeat the bands

D

of pattern exactly the same distance apart, so that they will correspond when fitted together. Brick-coloured wool is used for the warp, with madder red for the main part of the weft and nigger brown for the stripes. When the weaving is complete the two pieces are joined together. Tack them side by side on a piece of fairly stiff paper; the diagram shows the method

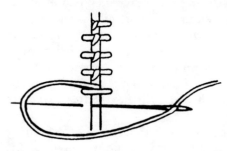

of stitching for which the brown wool is used. Bring the needle up on the left-hand piece of weaving, hold the thread under the thumb and pick up a piece on the edge of the right-hand piece, then take up a piece on the left, but this time not holding the thread under the thumb, and so on, picking up a piece first on the left edge and then on the right edge. When joined the weaving is folded into half and three or four thicknesses of felt, or some similar material, are inserted. The edges are tacked together, turning in the cut ends, after which the entire edge is sewn with brown buttonhole stitches arranged in groups of three (see Diagram 9, page 45). A buttonholed loop of brown wool can be added at one corner for hanging purposes if desired.

One 11-in. length of weaving on a 7-in. loom can be used for the kettle-holder, instead of two narrow braids, or the weaving can be done on a wide loom using only part of the width of the heddle.

PINCUSHION. (Illustrated on Plate 10.)

The weaving of this is the same as for the kettle-holder. The colours used are blue for the warp, with blue, grey and purple for the weft. The strips of weaving are sewn together, and the join decorated with purple herringboning. The weaving is folded into two and the edges joined together, leaving an opening for inserting the cushion. An inner case is made and filled with bran, and this is inserted in the woven cover, after

SOME USES FOR THE BRAIDS

which the opening is sewn up. Finally, a small woollen cord
or plait is sewn round the edge of the cushion to hide the join.
The ends of this are made into a loop for hanging purposes
at one corner.

Egg Cosy. (Illustrated on Plate 10.)

Two strips of weaving, 8½ in. long and 2 in. wide, made on a
small loom, are used for this cosy. Two colours of wool are
used for the warp: the centre group of strands are orange and
those on either side pale yellow. Deep yellow wool is used for
the main part of the weft and white for the small stripes.

The two strips of weaving are oversewn together with yellow
wool, then the weaving is folded in half and the outer corners
tucked inside, until only a distance of 1¾ in. of the fold remains
between. These edges and the side edges are joined by oversewing them with the yellow wool. The lower edges of the cosy
are turned under ready for padding and lining. Yellow felt is
used for the lining, with three thicknesses of wadding for
either side of the cosy. The wadding is cut the same size as the
cosy and oversewn at the edges, but turnings must be allowed
on the felt. Both are inserted inside the cosy, and the felt is
sewn to the weaving along the lower edge with overcast stitches
of yellow wool. Then it is secured at the top with a yellow,
pear-shaped wooden bead and a small round orange bead,
which also serve as a means of removing the cosy.

Shoe Polisher. (Illustrated on Plate 10.)

This is very useful to carry in one's handbag. It is in the form
of a small pocket or bag. The main back piece is of weaving
(see illustration), while the front pocket or pad piece is made
with double felt, so that the hand can be inserted for polishing.
When not in use it is rolled up and fastened with a loop and
bead. Two strips of weaving, 8½ in. long and 2 in. wide, are
used; this length allows for turnings. As mentioned in the two
previous examples, the weaving can be done in one continuous
length and cut into two pieces afterwards. Care must be taken
again to repeat the bands of pattern exactly so that they
correspond when fitted together. Dark green wool is used for

the warp, and apple green for the main part of the weft, with stripes of lime green and orange. When the weaving is complete the two strips are joined together in the same way as for the kettle-holder, using dark green wool. The polisher is completed as follows: cut a piece of green felt, 9 in. long and the same width of the weaving, fold it into half to make a double piece. Turn in the lower edge of the weaving and place the felt in position on it with the folded edge for the top of the pocket. Buttonhole the sides and bottom edges together with dark green wool. When complete, make a small hem at the top edge of the weaving, turn the corners down to the wrong side and sew them, leaving a $1\frac{1}{2}$-in. space between. This will form the shaped flap. Finally, buttonhole a small brass ring with dark green wool and sew it at the centre of the flap, allowing it to protrude half-way over the edge, and then roll the polisher up and find a suitable corresponding place to attach a wooden bead for fastening purposes. One piece of weaving $8\frac{1}{2}$ in. long and 4 in. wide, woven on a $5\frac{1}{2}$-in. loom, can be used instead of two narrow braids.

BABY'S BONNET. (Illustrated on Plate 12.)

The construction of this is quite simple. Three strips of weaving on the small loom, using the whole width of the heddle, are required. Two of the strips are all of white wool, while the centre one is striped with blue. They are each 14 in. long. When the weaving is complete, the strips are tacked on paper and joined with white wool, using the same stitch as in diagram on page 42. Then the weaving is taken off the paper and folded in half, and two of the edges joined together in the same way for the centre back of the bonnet. After this the top point of the centre is folded down for about $2\frac{1}{4}$ in. in the form of a triangle (see Diagram 8, page 45), and secured with a few buttonhole stitches. The lower edge of the bonnet is turned under $\frac{1}{2}$ in., and made into a narrow hem at each end for a distance of about $1\frac{1}{4}$ in., so that it is quite neat for turning back at the front of the bonnet. The 'turn back' measures $\frac{3}{4}$ in., and is buttonholed along the edge with blue wool. The bonnet is much nicer lined. A strip of silk is cut for the front portion

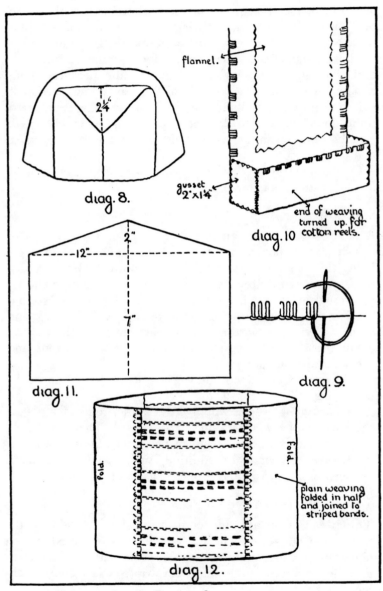

flannel.

2¼"

diag. 8.

gusset
2"×1¼"

end of weaving
turned up. for
cotton reels.

diag. 10

2"

12"

1"

diag. 11.

diag. 9.

fold.

fold.

plain weaving
folded in half
and joined to
striped bands.

diag. 12.

DIAGRAMS 8 TO 12.

of the bonnet and a square for the back. These are tacked in position inside the bonnet, letting the inner edge of the front piece wrap over the edges of the back square piece, but leaving the lower edge of the latter loose. Before tacking this the edge of the back square of weaving is pleated until it measures 2½ in., making two pleats on each side of the centre join, so that it will fit well under the baby's head. Then the lining is gathered up to this side and tacked, after which the lining can be sewn. Finally, ribbon strings are attached between the front turnover and the bonnet.

One 14-in. length of weaving on a 9-in. loom can be used instead of three narrow braids.

Sewing Case

A useful sewing case can be made from an 18-in. length of weaving, made on a 7-in. loom, as shown in Diagram 10. After lining the weaving, one end is folded up on the inside and a small gusset, 2 in. deep by 1¼ in. wide, of the lining material is inserted at each side to make a pocket for reels of cotton. A piece of flannel measuring approximately 8 in. long and 3½ in. wide is sewn on the inside of the remaining flat portion for needles. The case is rolled up and a buttonholed loop and a bead added for fastening.

Two lengths of weaving on a 3½-in. loom, joined down the centre, could be used instead.

The foregoing articles will give the worker some idea of how the various pieces of weaving can be used. They are by no means exhaustive. Below are given a few suggestions for weaving on the wider looms. In addition, such articles as scarves, runners, pyjama cases and slipper bags can be made.

Tea Cosy. (Illustrated on Plate 13.)

This is woven on a 15-in. loom, using the full width of the heddle. Twenty-one inches of weaving are required, which allows for turnings. Delphinium blue wool is used for the warp and the main part of the weft, with stripes of saxe blue, parchment and indigo.

When the weaving is complete it is folded into half, with the right side inside. A distance of 2 in. is measured down from the fold at the edges and joined with a line to the centre of the cosy to give the pointed top (see Diagram 11, page 45). The two sides are machined together along the side edges and the top. The turnings are pressed out as flat as possible, and the weaving turned on to the right side ready for lining. The lower edges are turned under first. Three layers of wadding are cut for each side of the cosy, the same size as this, and oversewn together at the edges. Then the lining, which is of blue felt, is cut out, leaving ½-in. turnings. The edges are sewn up, after which the wadding and the lining are inserted in the cosy. The lower edge of the wadding is slip-stitched into position, then the edge of the lining is turned under and secured to the weaving with blue wool buttonholing in groups of three stitches. Finally, a brass ring is buttonholed with the same coloured wool and secured to the point of the cosy, taking the stitches through to the lining to hold this in position.

CUSHION. (Illustrated on Plate 13.)

Four pieces of weaving on the 15-in. loom, using the full width of the heddle, are required for this cushion. Two of the pieces are striped and these are used for the centre of each side. The remaining two pieces, which are of plain weaving, are folded in half down their width and joined to the edges of the striped pieces so that the fold makes the edge of the cushion in each case (see Diagram 12, page 45).

The four pieces each measure 18 in. long, which allows for turnings.

Mercerised cotton is used double throughout; cinnamon brown for both the warp and the weft of the two plain strips, also for the warp of the striped pieces and the main part of the weft, with stripes of deep yellow, parchment and fawn.

When the weaving is complete, the pieces are joined together as already mentioned. The joins are decorated with deep yellow buttonholing in groups of three stitches, and small parchment loop-stitches in pairs between the groups. Finally, the ends are joined together, leaving a space for inserting the cushion.

BLOTTER. (Illustrated on Plate 13.)

This is also woven on a 15-in. loom with double mercerised cotton.

The weaving is folded and sewn into a cover or case, and a piece of cardboard covered with blotting paper is inserted in each side of the cover. The full width of the heddle is used and a piece of weaving 26 in. long is required. This allows for turnings in making up. In addition to this, four more inches of weaving are required to make a strap for the inside of the blotter to hold the blotting paper in position.

Yellow is used for the warp and deep yellow for the weft, with stripes of fawn and nigger brown.

When the weaving is complete it is lined on the inside with yellow linen. The side edges are turned under until the weaving is 12 in. wide and the lining and the weaving are oversewn together. The ends of the weaving are then folded back for 2½ in. and secured at the edges to make a pocket at each end for inserting the blotting pad. The strap for the inside is made double, the edges being turned in and sewn together so that it measures about 1½ in. wide when complete. It is placed across the centre; the ends are turned under and firmly sewn to the edges of the weaving.

The two pieces of cardboard for the pads are cut to fit exactly into the pockets, allowing sufficient room between them under the strap for the case to shut easily, but not too much or the weaving will be loose. Cover them with blotting paper, using a little paste. Insert them in the case, and then insert one or two sheets of blotting paper right across the two covers.

THE MAKING OF GARMENTS

The woven material on the wide looms, 15 in., 18 in. and 20 in., can be made into most attractive and useful garments, such as a skirt, jumper blouse, sleeveless cardigan, child's frock, tunic and knickers, dressing gown, etc. It is hardly practical to include illustrations of these here, because of the constant change of fashion, although the basis remains the same, e.g.

DRYAD

PLATE 13. Above: Blotter and Tea Cosy.
Below: Cushion.

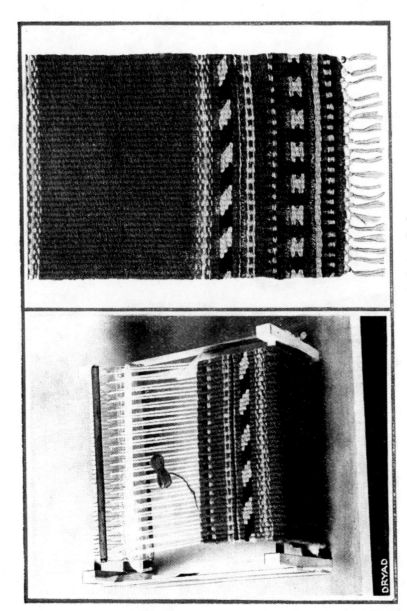

PLATE 14. Rug weaving on the large roller loom.

PLATE 15. Examples of work carried out at a weaving course for teachers at the Nottingham School of Art.

four widths of weaving on a 20-in. loom will make a skirt; two widths woven on a 15-in. loom will make the front of a cardigan or jumper, and two widths for the back. The sleeves of the jumper can be made with two more widths, one for the top half of the sleeve and one for the lower half. The main thing is to arrange for the joins to come in some suitable place; apart from this the garments are cut out just as any other materials. The joins can be made invisible by seaming the edges together on the wrong side with a machine, or where suitable they can be joined decoratively with embroidery stitches.

EXAMPLES OF WEAVING ILLUSTRATED ON PLATES 9, 11 AND 15

Some work done on the looms described at weaving courses specially arranged for teachers at the Leicester College of Art and the Nottingham School of Art has been included with the kind permission of the school authorities to show the standard of work to be attained by workers in a very short time without any previous experience. At the same time these examples give a number of interesting patterns and suggestions.

Plate 9. The upper half shows two pochettes. The one with the lightning fastener and the woollen tassel is made of three narrow braids woven on a 3½-in. loom and joined together. The other pochette is woven on a 15-in. loom, the width of the weaving being folded into three to make the depth of the pochette so that the bands of pattern run down it.

The tea cosy in the lower half is made up of strips of weaving done on a 5½-in. loom, two lengths being woven with a pattern for the lower edge of the cosy. Each side of the cosy has two and a half braids to make the depth, so that five lengths are required altogether. These, however, could be woven in one continuous length and cut up later.

Plate 11 shows a scarf and cushion, both of which were woven on a 15-in. loom.

E

The scarf in the upper half of the plate has a shaded warp, the lightest tone being at the centre, gradually shading to darker tones at the edges.

The cushion in the lower half is made of two pieces of weaving, joined together invisibly down the centre. In each piece the patterned border was carefully planned so that it would fit together and make a continuous band round the cushion, i.e. for the left half of the cushion; after completing a few inches of plain weaving for the lower edge of the cushion, the patterned border is woven across, beginning at the extreme edge on the right-hand side of the warp and terminating a few inches from the left-hand edge, the remaining portion being completed with plain weaving for the side edge of the cushion.

When the border is complete, plain weaving is begun at the right edge for the centre portion of the cushion and the patterned border continued at the left-hand side only, the width of this corresponding to the depth of the border just woven. The remainder of the row is completed with plain weaving, as before.

The weaving is continued in this manner until the depth of the plain centre portion of the cushion is complete, and then the border pattern is woven across for the top of the cushion and a few rows of plain weaving added for the edge.

The other half of the cushion is woven in exactly the same way, and when cut off the loom is turned round facing the first half ready for the edges to be joined together.

Plate 15. This group of weaving, mainly of scarves, shows simple striped and plaid patterns of plain weaving and borders of pattern weaving. These were all done by 'beginners' at a weaving course for teachers at the Nottingham School of Art. Various examples of fringing the warp strands are included here.

RUG WEAVING ON THE WIDER LOOMS

(15 in. to 20 in.)

These looms can be used for rug weaving. Door mats can be made and larger rugs by joining the pieces of weaving together.

Plate 14 shows a mat in progress on a 15-in. loom, while the finished mat is shown beside it, one end being folded under.

Soft cotton string is used for the warp, and in this instance a single-ply rug yarn was used for the weft. Other rug wools, three-ply or six-ply, can be used, the latter making a much thicker mat.

THE WARP

The warp is made in a very simple manner, for with this coarse weaving it is not necessary to make a cross to keep the warp in order, as in the finer form of weaving. The 15-in. loom will take $2\frac{1}{2}$ yards of the warp string conveniently, which will make two door mats 30 in. long and $13\frac{1}{2}$ in. wide, allowing for waste and contraction.

The warp strands require to be of double string and $\frac{3}{8}$ in. apart, so that in threading up the heddle a double strand is threaded into the first hole, and then instead of threading the second double strand in the next space, miss one space, one hole, one space, one hole, and thread it in the following *space*. Similarly, miss one hole, one space, one hole, one space, before threading the next double strand through the following *hole*, and repeat alternately in this manner across the heddle. This will leave two holes and two spaces between each of the warp strands.

Count the number of double strands required and cut them $2\frac{1}{2}$ yards long. Thread the heddle as described and tie the double warp strands round a stick in groups of two. Tie this stick to the back roller with string through the slits provided in the calico attached to the roller. Wind the warp on to this roller, being careful to keep an even tension on all the strands. Tie another stick to the other roller and then tie the ends of the double warp strands round this stick in twos.

TO WEAVE

The secret of good rug weaving lies in keeping the weft wool at the right tension. It should be left looser than in ordinary weaving so that it fits well round the warp strings and allows the rows of weaving to be pressed well down one upon the other, thus completely hiding the warp and giving a rich texture and thickness to the rug. It is not possible to obtain this tension by passing the weft thread across the warp in one movement as in ordinary weaving. It must only be passed through a small group of warp strands at a time, and as the wool is drawn through it should be left in an arched position rather than horizontal before it is pressed down into place with the fingers. Several movements are therefore necessary for each row.

Instead of lifting or pressing down the heddle to make a shed for each of these separate movements, after making the shed insert a stick broadways up so that it remains thus during the weaving of the whole of the row.

This stick can be used to beat the row in position before being removed in readiness for changing the shed with the heddle, after which it is inserted again for the next row.

The weft wool is used in lengths of two to three yards, and for convenience is wound as follows: leaving a short end, wind the wool backwards and forwards on the left hand between the thumb and little finger, making a cross at the centre. Loop the short end round the centre in the form of a buttonhole stitch or a half-hitch so that the long end can be easily drawn out. This 'bunch' of wool can then be passed through the warp strands conveniently with the fingers.

In introducing a new length of wool, leave an end of 3 in. or 4 in. of both the old and new wool. Secure these ends by threading them up the weaving by the side of the nearest warp string, when a few more inches of weaving have been done, or when the mat is finished.

It is advisable to begin the weaving with a few rows of the warp string. This helps to set the warp in order at the beginning and provides a firm foundation for the first few rows of wool weaving. The rows of string are repeated at the end to correspond with those at the beginning.

PATTERN WEAVING

The simplest form of pattern making is that of introducing rows of contrasting colour in some definite order, as in the other weaving, e.g. several alternate rows of two colours will give a series of squares similar to a chequer pattern, as at the ends of the mat illustrated.

Patterns are also made by weaving to and fro on groups of the warp strings with various colours, making definite shapes of colour fitting up to each other, as in the bands of pattern shown on the mat. Here the weaving can be done more simply without using the heddle to make the sheds, the warp strings being picked up with the fingers of the left hand as required, while the wool is passed through with the right hand. Starting at one edge, a portion of the first colour shape is woven according to pattern and then the colour immediately against it is introduced and woven up to the same level, and so on across the mat, continuing until the pattern is complete, following which it must be beaten up well with the stick or heddle.

When the weaving is complete it is removed from the loom by cutting the warp strings close to the knots which tied them into the calico. The double warp strings are then knotted together in pairs close to the weaving, after which they are divided and different pairs knotted together again a short distance below to form a fringe.

To make a rug 27 in. wide by 60 in. long, two strips of weaving, 60 in. long, are woven and joined together with a lacing stitch of wool. The join can be made invisible, or decorative, according to the colour of wool used. Another method of making a rug would be to join four small mats together side by side with the joins running across the width.

It may be helpful for the worker to know that 2½ oz. of the cotton string is required for the warp of the mat given, with 9½ oz. of the single-ply wool, or 14 oz. of the six-ply wool.

SOME DRYAD BOOKS

THE WEAVER'S CRAFT. By L. E. SIMPSON, B.A., Lecturer in Crafts at the University of Birmingham, and M. WEIR, Examiner to the National Froebel Union. Crown quarto, 10 in. by 7½ in. Illustrated in colour, and with line diagrams and numerous photographs. 148 pages. Cloth boards. New edition ready Spring, 1936. 10s. 6d.

The book aims at giving a comprehensive account of weaving in all its forms and in a variety of materials from the simplest work for six-year-old children to the more advanced work on the hand loom with four heddles and six pedals. It is intended for all interested in the craft, but, in view of the value of this branch of handwork in education, special attention has been given to the needs of teachers. The first practical exercises deal with simple weaving, using paper, felt and raffia. The idea of pattern is next introduced, and horizontal and vertical stripes, plaids, simple 'all-over' patterns are mentioned in connection with the making of bags, pochettes, needlecases, etc. The many useful articles that can be made at this stage of simple appliance, such as lavender bottles, straw table mats, felt rugs, etc., are also described. The preparation of wool for weaving—scouring, spinning and dyeing—is next dealt with, followed by a chapter on the invention of labour-saving weaving devices and their application to hand-made looms. Rug-weaving is next dealt with in some detail, and there follow chapters on the simple roller loom, the four-heddle loom, the table loom, and the full-size loom. These latter chapters contain instructions for pattern reading and drafting together with many actual pattern drafts. The historical sequence of the development of the craft has been followed in the grading of the work, and explicit working instructions are given at every stage.

TABLET WEAVING. By MABEL W. PEACH. 8 pages of half-tone illustrations and 24 diagrams. 28 pages. Paper covers. 1s. 0d.

This is an important practical work on the subject, very cleverly concentrated into booklet form. It has an interesting introduction, giving a vivid account of the craft in many lands. The technical instruction is sound and simply put before the reader.

The writer justly claims that this craft is especially suited to the needs of both the amateur and of school children, not only on account of the slightness and inexpensiveness of the apparatus, but also for the variety of charming uses to which it may be applied. In England and the United States tablet weaving is being used for Occupational Therapy. Apart from this it makes an excellent

Printed in the United States
127760LV00001B/87/A

9 781406 799651